# The Ultimate Pilgrimage for

# Catholic Youth

## By Sharon M. Gagne

## Sunshine~Life Sgagne

# Name

_____

# My World Youth Day Pilgrimage

## to:_____

## Dates:_____

# This book is dedicated to:

**Florence Marie Nardozzi**

**(Grammy)**

**She always believed in me, and I know she watches over me each day.**

**And**

**Charlotte Antoinette Gagne**

**(Mom)**

# Acknowledgements:

First and foremost, I thank God. He has been my guide and inspiration throughout the creation of this book.

I also want to thank those who have read through this book as it was in production. I thank them for their input, ideas, and suggestions. I also thank them for making sure I take a break in my thoughts and use a comma. Thanks to Mom (Charlotte Gagne), Virginia Goncela, Hayley Wigul, Trish Charmut, Shawnee Baldwin, Grisell Fernzandez, Jenny and Raul Santiago, and Linda Podos. Thank you also to my Dad, who is always there to help with the numbers.

To Roberta Murphy (Bert) the youth minister, who took me on my first World Youth Day. Thank you to all the teens and youth ministers that have come with me on the various World Youth Days. You have given me stories to talk and write about.

# Table of Contents

12

# Introduction

"Awesome!" "Exciting!" "Invigorating!" are just some of the words I would use to describe World Youth Day. Saint Pope John Paul II started the event in 1984. He wanted to get youth (eighteen and above, until 1993, when it changed to sixteen and above) from around the world to join to share and celebrate their faith. He invited youths to join him in Rome, Italy, in 1985 for the first World Youth Day. World Youth Day is celebrated each year in dioceses around the world. Every three years there is an International World Youth Day. (For previous locations of International World Youth Days, see Appendix A.)

Let me begin by telling you a little about myself and how I came to know about World Youth Day. I grew up in a Catholic home and attended Catholic schools from grades one through twelve. Yes, I wore a uniform for most of my childhood and adolescence. They are not as bad as you think. You get to sleep in a little later each day because you know what you are going to wear. In high school I became involved in the youth group at my church. I enjoyed going to all the activities, community services, and events. I especially enjoyed the retreats we would attend. The biggest retreat/pilgrimage for me was World Youth Day 1993. Ever since then, I have been hooked. I have been involved in youth ministry for over thirty years. In addition to being a youth minister, I am a licensed professional counselor who works with children and adolescents every day. I have had many experiences working with youth, and they have also taught me a lot about faith.

As I said earlier, my first World Youth Day was in 1993, and I vividly remember getting on the plane to Denver, Colorado. This was the beginning of an experience I would remember for the rest of my life. The energy and the excitement on the plane was awesome. The whole plane was filled with pilgrims from our archdiocese. I remember the bishop getting on the PA system and saying a prayer for a safe journey before we took off. While in flight, he also led us in the rosary. Can you imagine a whole plane saying the rosary? This was a very holy plane, for sure.

The day we left for the pilgrimage was already a special day for me. It was August 10, my birthday. My youth minister told the bishop, and he had the whole plane sing "Happy Birthday" to me. Pretty cool!

Every time I attend a World Youth Day, I grow deeper in my faith and pilgrim travel. Since my first World Youth Day in 1993 as a youth participant in Denver, I have been eager to share the experience with others. I have taken youths to World Youth Days in Toronto, Canada; Cologne, Germany; Sydney, Australia; Madrid, Spain; Rio de Janeiro, Brazil and Krakow, Poland. In Australia, Madrid, Rio, Krakow. I had the great opportunity to lead catechesis (see chapter 6 for more information) for three days. I had the pleasure  of working with bishops from— England, Australia, Bangladesh,  United States,  Ghana and  Philippines.to name a few. Together we ministered to youths from countries that I had never even heard of. As I update this book, I am preparing for World Youth Day 2019 in Parana City, Panama

I have written this book not only for you, a youth participant, but also for youth ministers and/or adults who will be accompanying youth on the pilgrimage. It is divided into three parts. The first section is for youth participants. The second section is a journal, which is a space for you to write about your experiences and to share with others when you return home. This journal is a keepsake of your great spiritual journey. The third section is for youth ministers or adult who are planning for World Youth Day and accompanying pilgrims to World Youth Day.

This book will give you tips on getting the most out of your experience, taking into account the points of view of both a youth minster and youths who have already attended a World Youth Day. I suggest you read through this book before you go and refer to it as a guide each day. You'll find a section on what to pack, which you may want to read now, so you can start collecting the things you will need. If you don't have a sleeping bag, for example, you could ask for one as a Christmas, confirmation, graduation, or birthday gift.

At the end of each chapter there will be three symbols:

    ✦   A journal question for you to reflect on  for that chapter
    ☼   A handy tip for you
    ╫   A Bible quote to reflect on

Finally, once you have read this book yourself, give it to your parents to read so that they can gain a better understanding of the wonderful opportunity that you are going to be experiencing. God Bless.

# See you at the next World Youth Day.

# Sharon

# Chapter 1: Preparing

Congratulations! You have taken a great step toward deepening your faith by committing to go to World Youth Day. You are going to have an awesome pilgrimage. A pilgrimage, according to Webster's, is "a journey of a pilgrim to a shrine or sacred place" (Webster, 1989). Before you go any further, I would like you to take a few minutes to answer the following questions about the pilgrimage you are embarking on.

- Why do you want to go to World Youth Day?
- How do you feel about attending World Youth Day?
- What expectations do you have?
- What concerns do you have?

- Journal: Now turn to chapter 1 in the journal section.

☼ *Tip: Pray each day about the pilgrimage you are about to embark on.*

✝ "God alone is my rock and my salvation, my secure height; I shall not fall." (Psalm 62:3)

# Chapter 2: Fund-raising

Fund-raising may be one of the hardest parts of your journey. The World Youth Day (WYD) Sydney 2008's official souvenir guide featured an article about the fund-raising efforts of a young girl from Papua, New Guinea. It stated: "She started her fund-raising efforts in 2006 by selling bananas. From that she made enough to buy a bag of peanuts to sell. Then she bought vegetable seeds to plant. Once she sold the veggies, she bought chicks to rear and sell. By her third batch of fifty-two chickens—and a pig for good measure—she fully raised her air travel" (Hunter, 2008).

Fund-raising is hard work and time-consuming, but it can also be a lot of fun. It is a great way to build a relationship with the other participants who will be going to World Youth Day with you. It's easy to get frustrated when some of the people in your group aren't working as hard as everyone else. So, it is important that you do your part. Take a leadership role and offer to head up one of the fund-raisers. Get your parents, brothers, sisters, aunts, uncles, and friends involved.

Ideas for fund-raisers:

- Dances at your church
- Car washes
- Tag sales
- Bake sales & jewelry sales
- Gift card sales for a local grocery store

➢ Sell clothing with your church name and logo on it. (Wear these clothes to WYD, and have parishioners wear theirs too while you are away, so that they will remember to pray for you.)

➢ Sponsorship program, in which a parishioner sponsors a pilgrim for a specific sum. In return, the parishioner receives a gift from World Youth Day. You can get a discount on World Youth Day items from its official Web site. For several World Youth Days, we had four sponsor levels: a $25 sponsorship received a gift of a WYD rosary; $50, a WYD candle; $75, a WYD tote bag; and $100, a WYD T-shirt. Each member who sponsored us wrote their name on a banner, which we brought to World Youth Day to be blessed by the Pope. We have displayed this banner in our church. When we returned, we had a special reception for the sponsors and showed them a slide show of our pilgrimage. Talk to your youth minster about this fund-raising option.

✦ Journal: As you are doing your fund-raising, go to chapter 2 in your journal to write about your experiences. You may also want to brainstorm ideas on fund-raisers there also.

☼ *Tip: Do your part of the fund-raising. Use the chart on the next pages to track your fund-raising and when your payments are due.*

✠ "Entrust your works to the Lord, and your plans will succeed." (Proverbs 16:3)

**Payment Breakdown**

**Total $**_____

| Payments | Amount | Date Due | Date Paid |
|---|---|---|---|
| *Deposit* | | | |
| *1ˢᵗ Payment* | | | |
| *2ⁿᵈ Payment* | | | |
| *3ʳᵈPayment* | | | |
| *4ᵗʰ Payment* | | | |
| *Final Payment* | | | |
| | | | |

*© 2011,2016, 2018 Sharon M. Gagne*

## Fund-raisers

| Type | Date | How Much Raised | My Portion |
|------|------|-----------------|------------|
|      |      |                 |            |
|      |      |                 |            |
|      |      |                 |            |
|      |      |                 |            |
|      |      |                 |            |
|      |      |                 |            |

*© 2011, 2016, 2018 Sharon M. Gagne*

# Chapter 3: What to Pack

The location of World Youth Day will dictate some items you'll need to pack, so you'll want to know the weather for the location you are going. Go to www.weather.com (The Weather Channel, 1995-2010) to look up the weather for the location.

## Items Needed

**(Put a check in the sun ☼ when you've got it packed.)**

☼ **Comfortable Backpack**—Try the backpack on to make sure it is comfortable. You will be carrying it daily and for long durations.

☼ **Suitcase**—Check with the airlines on size limitations. You can also get an FAA lock for your suitcase.

☼ **Socks and Underwear**—A pair for each day.

☼ **T-shirts**—Check with your youth minister if you are getting T-shirts made with your parish name. The dress for World Youth Day is pretty much casual, but check with your youth minister to see if something else is needed.

☼ **Sweatshirt or Jacket**—It gets cool at night.

- ☼ **Pants**—It can be chilly. Also, your legs need to be covered in order to go into some churches.
- ☼ **Shorts**—Bring neutral colors; they go with everything. Make sure they are the right length. When your arms are by your side, your fingertips should touch the hem.
- ☼ **Sneakers**—*Do not* bring new ones. Make sure they are well broken in before you go. You will be doing a lot of walking each day, and you do not want blisters.
- ☼ **Toiletries**—If you are going to bring them on the plane, make sure they are FAA-approved size. Check the Web site at www.faa.gov.
- ☼ **Antibacterial Gel**—There may not be places to wash your hands all the time

- ☼ **PBA-Free Water Bottle**—Get a carbineer so you can just clip your water bottle on your backpack and not have to carry it.
- ☼ **Small Roll of Toilet Paper**—You never know when you might need it. ☺
- ☼ **Sleeping Bag**—This is for the overnight and also for those who have simple accommodations. Check out its weight, because you will have to carry it to the pilgrimage site.
- ☼ **Feminine Hygiene Products**—Ladies, you do not know how products in other countries will work with your body. Be prepared with your own supplies.

- ☼ **Pens and Sharpies**
- ☼ **Rain Poncho**—They can be purchased at local department stores. I have used them not only for the rain but also to put on the ground to sit on if it is wet.
- ☼ **Umbrella for the Rain and the Sun**—While waiting for events, the sun can get hot, and there may not be any shade. You can also use the umbrella to help find your group. If one member holds up the umbrella, others can find where the group is sitting. You can decorate the group's umbrellas so they are easy to spot.
- ☼ **Bandana**—This has many uses. It can be used to keep your head cool, to help tie things together, or to tie on your backpack to indicate your group's bags.
- ☼ **Flashlight and Batteries**—For the vigil and walking home at night
- ☼ **Sunscreen and Bug Spray**
- ☼ **Medicine**—Make sure your youth minister knows what you take in case of emergency. Take your medicine with you each day if you have to take it daily. Once you leave your hotel in the morning, you will not be back until the evening.
- ☼ **Tarp**—This is to put on the ground and/or to cover you at the overnight. More details will follow in the overnight section.
- ☼ **Resalable Plastic Bags and Empty Trash Bags**—Thousands of creative uses.
- ☼ **Bungee Cord and Carabineers**—They are great to attach things to your backpack or suitcase.

- ☼ **Portable AM/FM Radio**—At World Youth Day they will broadcast the events on different channels in different languages. The radio will help you know what is happening.
- ☼ **Camera**—A must have.
- ☼ **Rosaries**
- ☼ **Snack Food**—Check with the host country to see what food they allow. When we went to Australia, they did not let us bring any food with us because it is an island. Things that you might want to bring are granola bars (minus the chocolate ones; when they melt, you will have a mess in your bag), flavored water packets, crackers, protein bars, and a jar of peanut butter (great source of protein).
- ☼ **Money**—You will want to get currency for the country you are going to. Visit a local bank to get info about it. Another thing you can get is a Visa Travel debit card. You can put money on it in your currency and use it in a debit card machine in the country World Youth Day is in. Then you can take out the money in their currency. You will be charged a fee for it. But if you use your own bank ATM, you will be charged a fee from the ATM and another from your bank. With the Visa card, it is just one fee.
- ☼ **Items to Trade**—Pins, key rings, postcards, bookmarks, bracelets, or prayer cards. Another idea is to get a deck of playing cards with your hometown on it. You can give one card out to each person you meet. (This idea came from another youth minister, Steve.)
- ☼ **Extra Bag**—Many of you will be trading things with others and collecting treasures along the way. With airlines charging for each bag, I suggest bringing a foldable duffle bag in your suitcase. A few in your group can put everything inside it and then share the cost of the bag on the flight.

☼ **Bathing Suit**

☼ **Electrical Adapter**—Each country is different; check for what you need before you go.

☼ **Health Insurance Information**—You and your youth minister should each have a copy of your health insurance card.

☼ **Your Passport and Visa**—Bring your originals with you but make two copies before you leave. Give one to your parents to keep at home and put a second copy in your suitcase.

☼ **Immunizations**—You will want to check with your youth minister to see if any are needed for the country that you will be entering.

☼ **THIS BOOK**

⊹ Journal: As you are packing for your pilgrimage, turn to chapter 3 in your journal.

☼ *Tip: You do not need to bring your whole closet with you. Pack light, because you will be carrying your own things.*

⊹ "Let no one have contempt for your youth, but set an example for those who believe in speech, conduct, love, faith, and purity." (1 Timothy 4:12)

# Chapter 4: Getting Ready to Go

As you are getting ready to go, a ton of things are flowing through your mind. You are excited, but also a little worried. One thing many teens who go on the pilgrimage worry about is what is going to happen at home while they are gone—situations with families, friends, boyfriends, girlfriends, and so forth. You are embarking on a spiritual experience of a lifetime. One thing that you will want to do is to be fully present at WYD. I know with e-mail, texting and twittering, this may be hard to do, because you will want to keep in contact with everyone at every moment at home. You will be gone a week or maybe two. Unless there is an emergency, I recommend limiting your communication with home (your dog, cat, boyfriend, or girlfriend will survive), so you can be fully present to experience the great things God has planned for you. Your youth minister will set up an emergency phone contact tree with families at home and send e-mails to them.

**Important Things to Know**

You are going to be tired!

You are going to be sore!

You are going to want to whine and complain!

You are going to be inspired!

You are going to grow spiritually!

You are going to be among millions who share in your faith!

Way cool!

## Transportation

To get to World Youth Day, you may have to take a few modes of transportation. When we went to Toronto, Canada, we took a bus. To make time go by, we played games and watched movies. When we went to Australia, it took us three planes to get there and four to come home. We brought along books, card games, and travel games; and we made crafts to trade with youths from other countries. Your youth minister will know in advance how long the traveling will be, so plan accordingly. Get a copy of your travel plans from your youth minister in case you get separated. When traveling by plane, you will need to go through security screening at the airport. Check with the Federal Aviation Administration about the items that you cannot travel with at the time of your flight.

## Once You Arrive

If you fly, you will have to go through customs when you reach the country you are going to. You will need to fill out paperwork. Your youth minister can help you with that. Be patient, because going through customs can take a while.

## Sleeping Arrangements

For World Youth Day, different kinds of sleeping arrangements are available to pilgrims. Some include simple housing, such as staying in a school, local church, or a host home. Others will be staying at various hotels or hostels.

We have stayed in hotels for each of the World Youth Days that I have gone to. When you get to your hotel, get familiar with your surroundings. Make sure you know where exits are in an emergency. Write down the room number of your youth minister so you have it in case of emergency.

Your youth minster will be giving you a World Youth Day backpack with lots of things in it. First and most important are the credentials that you must wear all week long. They will be your entrance ticket to events. You will also be given tickets for the major events, as well as your meal tickets for the week. Put them in a safe place. Do not lose them. In the backpack will also be a book with maps of the city, transportation info, and youth festival info, plus a lot of goodies.

## Food

Be open to new foods. When I was in Germany for WYD, I tried a chocolate spread called Nutella; it was fantastic. So, when I was in Australia, they had a spread called Vegemite; it was a brown color that looked something like chocolate. I thought it might be like the Nutella,

but when I tried it, it was so not the sweet taste of chocolate. It was a great topic of conversation for the week. In Madrid we were introduced to Churros and Chocolate. It was a great combination.

In Rio we tried several different types fruits for the first times some of them were Mangos and Papayas. We all came back with a new favorite fruit.

✦ Journal: As you are traveling, go to chapter 4 of your journal section and write about your traveling adventures.

☼ *Tip: When you travel, sometimes unexpected delays and problems may arise. Your youth minister will be working to make your trip as smooth as possible, but some things are out of their control. The best thing you can do is to not whine or complain, and to offer helpful thoughts and suggestions.*

╫ "Trust in God at all times, my people! Pour out your hearts to God our refuge." (Psalm 62:9)

# Chapter 5: Opening Ceremony

☼ Before you leave your hotel, check your journal to see what you need to bring with you today.

## Opening Ceremonies

Opening ceremonies can be held in a variety of places. Sometimes they are in a coliseum (Denver) , in a ballpark (Cologne), in an open area  (Sydney) or on a beach like Copacabana in Rio. The opening ceremony is the beginning of the week together. There will be singing, speakers, dancing, icebreakers, and Mass. It *will be* crowded. You will want to be prepared if you are going to have to sit on the ground. I would suggest putting down a tarp for your group and putting all your bags together. Make sure someone always stays with your things. Discuss with your youth minister a place to meet if you get separated. As you are waiting for events to start, mingle with others from other countries. Get to know them. Here you can begin trading items with new friends. You can list them in Appendix B and C. Once things start, the energy level of the pilgrims is going to be out of this world.

## World Youth Day Meals

Tonight, you will experience your first World Youth Day meal. They have had some different meal arrangements at World Youth Day. In Denver and Toronto, they issued each person a meal ticket for each meal. They then asked you to put together six tickets and send one person to get the food. They had one meal selection that everyone would have for their meal. In Madrid they gave you meal voucher that was accepted at various restaurants around the city. Those restaurants would have pilgrim menu that you would choose from. In Rio, they provided debt cards that allowed you to eat a specially designed WYD restaurants and food. In Poland there were vouchers given that you were able to turn in at different food tents for meals.

At World Youth Day be opened to try new foods.   You may come to like them (I loved Tim Tams in Australia).

At some meals there may be a boxed meal.  If you do not want something, (I do not like tuna fish), see if another person in your group or a nearby group wants it. Some of the food items you might want to keep for later are fruit, granola bars, rolls, and water. Those resalable plastic bags I told you to bring will come in handy now.

## Reconciliation

At the opening ceremony venue, there usually is a place for Reconciliation for you to go to, if you wish. There will be opportunities for you each day at the different venues, if you cannot go today.

## Restrooms

If you need to use the restrooms, go with someone and make sure your youth minister knows. Be prepared to wait in line. As a girl, the lines are usually longer, but I have found while waiting in line, you get to meet a lot of people from many different countries and strike up great conversations. Bring with you that extra toilet paper you have in your backpack, in case they run out.

## World Youth Day Theme Song

Tonight, you will hear the Theme song for this World Youth Day. It will be played and sung many times during the week. You may also hear previous World Youth Day theme songs. In Denver, I remember being in Mile High Stadium when Saint Pope John Paul II arrived in a helicopter and landed at the stadium. Dana Rosemary Scallon (known as just Dana) had written the theme song for the 1993 World Youth Day, "We Are One Body." They had the words up on a big screen, and the whole stadium was singing as Saint JPII was on the stage. Since then, I have sung this song many times at church, youth events, and at other World Youth Days.

(Mile High Stadium, Denver 1993)

When I asked Steve, who came with me to Sydney, what his most memorable experience from World Youth Day was, he said, "The most memorable was the first time you see all of the people. hundreds of thousands of people walking to their destinations waving their countries' flags, totally awesome!"

## Things to Buy

Merchandise stands will be set up at many of the venues. They will be selling religious items and items with the World Youth Day logo on them.

+ Journal: You will see and experience a lot of cool things. There will be a lot of miracles and works of Jesus around you. At the end of the day, turn to chapter 5 in your journal to reflect on your day and the ways that you have seen Jesus today.

☼ *Tip: Be open to meeting new people and having new experiences.*

⊹ "For where two or three are gathered in my name, there am I in the midst of them." (Matthew 18:20)

# Chapter 6: Catechesis & Day 1, 2, & 3 & Youth Festivals

☼ Before you leave your hotel, check your journal to see what you need to bring with you today.

For the next three days, you will be attending catechesis, which will teach you about your faith. It may be held in an arena, hall, convention center, or church. There will be speakers, singers, musicians, games, and skits. You will be assigned a site. Each day a different bishop will speak with you about the theme of the day, which will stem from the theme of World Youth Day.

I had the privilege of leading the catechesis for World Youth Day in Sydney, Madrid, Rio, and Krakow. In Sydney, our venue was held at Sacred Heart Catholic Church in Mosman. In Madrid, we were at old theatre that was turned in a church called Parish Neuestra Senora del Rosario de Filipinas, and in Rio we were in a church called Paroquia Nossa Senhora Aparecida. In Sydney, I had thirteen pilgrims, including me, who traveled each day out of Sydney to this church to worship and pray with youth from around the world. When I originally signed up to serve as an "animator"

(that is a term they use for host) for morning catechetical sessions, I was not sure what I was getting myself and my young adults into. I told my group that "God has a plan for us, and something great is going to happen." And boy, did it!

We made the church in Monson our home for three days to worship and pray. The first day, even though we were about ten minutes from beginning, not many people were in the church. Other members of my animation team said to me, "Where are all the people?" I said, "I don't know, but we will minister to those who are here." I went into the sanctuary to get a few things. When I came out, about three hundred people were there, and more kept filing in. God is good. ☺

The energy and spirit of the people who came to our catechesis was awesome. Every member who came with me had a role in the catechesis, from singers, readers, greeters, video tapers, and computer operators. We were in need of a keyboard player, and another youth minster from Greeley, Colorado, played with us. Many people who were at the catechesis asked how long we had all been working together. They even wanted to buy our CD. I told them we had only been playing together two days. How great God is to pull us all together.

While at World Youth Day, we blogged and uploaded videos from our catechesis. This was my first time using a flip video camera, and let's just say I got some tight close-ups of me at the beginning. As the week went on, I got better using the camera. The following site ( www.sunshinelife.net) has some video clips of the pilgrims at our catechesis singing the song "Lean on Me

Another cool thing about being the host of a catechesis is working with bishops from different countries. I had the great privilege to work with the Most Reverend Patricio Buzon, the bishop of

Kabankalan, Philippines; the Most Reverend Julian Porteous, auxiliary bishop of Syndey, Australia; Rt Reverend Bernard Longley, auxiliary bishop of Westminister, UK; Most Reverend Moses Costa, Bishop from Bangladesh, Most Reverend Samuel, Archbishop of Denver, Most Reverend Gabriel Charles Palmer-Buckle from Archbishop of Ghana, Most Reverend Edward James Burns. Bishop Juneau, Alaska, Cardinal Sean Patrick O' Malley from Boston, Massachusetts, Archbishop Christopher Prowse of Canberra-

(above) The Most Rev Julian Porteous Auxiliary Bishop of Sydney, Australia

(right) Rt Rev Bernard Longley Auxiliary Bishop of Westminster, UK.

Goulburn England and Auxiliary Bishop Robert Barron from Los Angles, California.

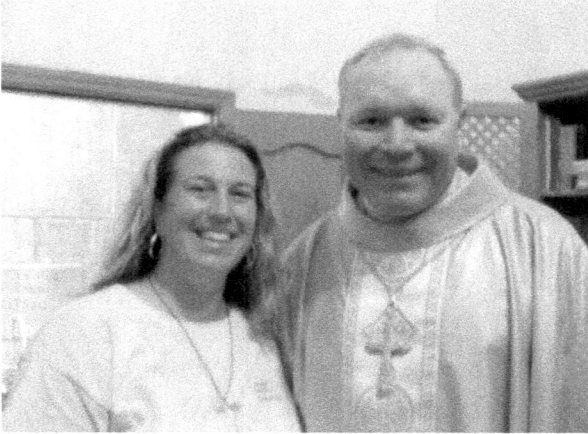

Each day I worked with a different bishop. The bishops spoke to the pilgrims about the themes of the day. They also had a question and answer session with the young people there. When you go, this will be your chance to ask a bishop a question that you always wanted to know. So, start thinking.

Each catechesis day will be different, though you will celebrate Mass each day. When you go to your catechesis each day, go with an open mind and heart; you will be amazed what God has in store for you.

(Top) Most Rev Edward James Burns of Bishop of Juneau, Alaska)

(Right) Most Rev Patricio Buzon, the Bishop of Kabankalan, Philippines,

(Right )Most Rev Gabriel Charles Parlmer Buckle Archbishop of Ghana ( Below) Archbishop of Canberra-Goulburn Most Rev Christopher Prowse

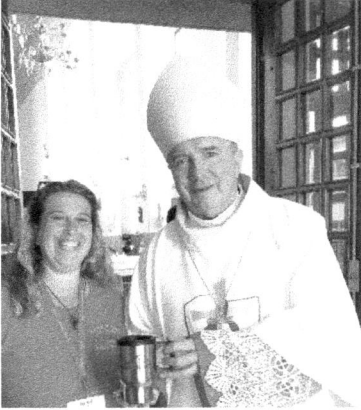

## Youth Festivals

Each day after your catechesis, you will attend different youth events around the city. When you get your World Youth Day program book with all the events, look it over to see what catches your eye and what draws your interest. Be open to see or hear something you might not hear back at home. Some things that will be available are talks, plays, visit to churches, adorations, and concerts.

When I was in Germany, we were on our way to a concert and stopped by a church called St. Michael. They were having adoration in the basement, and a single rose was present near the monstrance. There was something special about that church. Each member of the pilgrimage group who came with us felt that. After I was done with adoration, I began to walk around the church looking at the statues. There was a beautiful statue of Mary with candles all around it. As I was praying in front of it, I noticed an old-fashioned baby carriage. I turned to peek at the baby and noticed it was not a baby. It was an adult woman with a childlike body. That evening, when we were reflecting with our group on the day, I mentioned to our group about the baby carriage, but no one else had seen it or the woman in it. We prayed for the woman that night. But unbeknown to me, that would not be the end of the story. More to come…

✢ Journal: As you wrap up each day of catechesis, go to the chapter 6 sections of your journal to reflect on the message from the bishops for the day and to write about the youth festivals you went to and how they made you feel.

☼ *Tip: Thank all the volunteers that you see. So many people are giving their time to make this a great experience for you. Be sure to thank them. We had a great volunteer named Yanka who helped us with little details each day at our catechesis. She rocked!*

✚ "Shout joyfully to the Lord, all you lands; worship the LORD with cries of gladness; come before him with joyful song" (Psalm 100:1)

# Chapter 7: The Arrival of the Pope

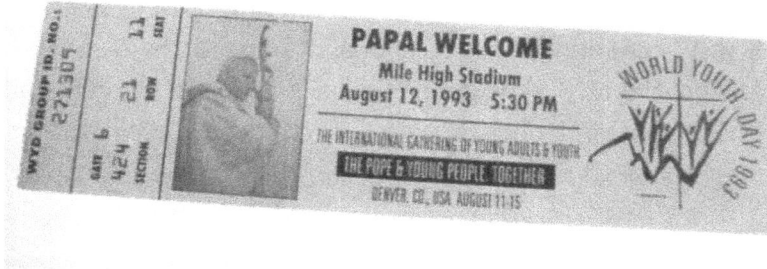

Today is the first day you will be able to see the Holy Father. When the Pope arrives at World Youth Day, he may come in a variety of ways. When Saint Pope John Paul II arrived in Denver and Toronto, it was in a helicopter. When Pope Benedict arrived in Cologne and Sydney, it was on the river in a huge boat. In Rio, Pope Francis drove along Copacabana beach in the Pope mobile. In past World Youth Day, you were given a ticket to a particular section for your group to be in. In Madrid and Rio there was no particular section assigned. In Krakow there were sections that you were assigned to. It will be crowded, so try to get there early and have your group find a spot. Other groups will be doing the same thing. This is a time when you can mingle with youth from other places and trade items.

When I asked Lauren, a youth who came with me, about the most unique item she traded, she said, "I traded one of my St. James shirts for a recycle club shirt from Wyoming. I still wear it today, and even though it has nothing to do with religion, every time I wear it, I kind of wonder if this girl in Wyoming knows she helps me get dressed in the morning, and it reminds me of the whole experience again every time I put it on."

In Denver, as we were waiting for the Pope's arrival at Mile High Stadium, it began to rain. We all broke out our handy dandy rain ponchos. We continued to sing and dance, despite the rain, as we awaited the arrival. Just as the Pope was arriving in the helicopter, the rain stopped, and a beautiful rainbow appeared above the stadium. God is awesome!

In Toronto, we were fortunate and were near the stage when Saint Pope John Paul II arrived. (See picture above)

In Germany we sat along the shore waiting for the boat with Pope Benedict to arrive. The banks were long, and we were not sure

where to sit. We finally found a spot under some trees. When the boat with the Pope on it came down the river, it went past where we were sitting. Then all of a sudden, it backed up and stopped right in front of our group.

In Sydney we waited for the Pope Benedict's  arrival at a place called Farm Cove.  It was by the water near the Sydney Opera House. There we joined up with a group from Malaysia, who taught us a few songs.

Others from our group taught some people from Italy how to make friendship bracelets, while some played a game of cards with new friends from other countries. When the Pope arrived, he came on a big boat. The pilgrims were yelling and cheering. They were also waving flags. The Pope disembarked from the boat, and he rode through the streets in his Pope mobile.

In Rio we were very fortunate to have the hotel we were staying at right along the Copacabana beach route that Pope Francis would be driving along. We were able to see him right from our hotel balcony. Pope Francis stopped

many times along the way to shake hands, kiss babies and talk to pilgrims.

✦ Journal: As you conclude your day, go to the chapter 7 part of your journal to reflect on the arrival of the Pope today.

☼ *Tip: Waiting for the Pope to come can be long but worth the wait. To make time pass, see how many people from different countries you can meet today.*

╬ "Amen, Amen I say to you, whatever you ask the Father in my name he will give you." (John 16:23)

# Chapter 8: Stations of the Cross

The stations of the Cross have been presented a variety of ways. Some have been set up across the city and others in one area. Big screens are often set up so that you can see what is happening at the other locations.

## Stations of the Cross

1. Jesus is condemned to death

2. Jesus takes up his cross

3. Jesus falls the first time

4. Jesus meets his mother

5. Simon helps Jesus carry his cross

6. Veronica wipes the face of Jesus

7. Jesus falls the second time

8. Jesus encounters the women of Jerusalem

9. Jesus falls the third time

10. Jesus is stripped of his garments

11. Jesus is nailed to the cross

12. Jesus dies on the cross

13. Jesus is taken down from the cross

14. Jesus is laid in the tomb

- Journal: After seeing the Stations of the Cross, go to chapter 8 of your journal section to reflect on the day.

☼ *Tip: Watching the Stations of the Cross can be emotional for some of your group. Be supportive of one another.*

✠ "Do not be afraid. I am the first and the last, the one who lives. Once I was dead, but now I am alive forever and ever. I hold the keys to death and the netherworld." (Revelations 1:17-18)

# Chapter 9: Pilgrimage

## Before You Go

OK, before you begin your pilgrimage, I hope you figured out how you are going to carry what you need today. Bungee cords and duct tape are your best friends. This is a test of your mind, body, and soul. As you head out with your group, stay together; millions of people are all going to the same place. Drink lots of water. Keep hydrated. Remind one another to drink. Offer to fill other group members' water bottles. Remember to be nice to your youth minster and to thank her/him for bringing you on this spiritual journal.

## Pilgrimage Route

So, you ask, where will you be walking? Each pilgrim route for World Youth Day has been very different. In the course of your walk, you may travel through city streets, through fields, through neighborhoods, along a highway and on a beach.

As we were walking in Germany, one of our pilgrims, who was walking in front of our group holding the flag, suddenly stopped and waited for me to reach her. She had a puzzled look on her face. She said to me, "Remember the other night when you told us about the woman in the baby carriage you saw?" I said yes. She said, "I wasn't sure what to make of that story but look over there. Is that the carriage you were speaking of?" It was, and the lady was in it, having lunch with her pilgrim group and laughing. We looked at each other and smiled. We continued to walk to catch up with our group. That night we shared with our group how we saw the lady again. We talked about the challenges she must face, but also the courage she has to make such a pilgrimage. But that was not the end of the story of the baby carriage. More to come.

## Arriving at the Vigil Site

When you reach the vigil site, you will be directed to your group section. Once you get there, you have to set things up. Put a tarp on the ground before putting your sleeping bag down. This will prevent your sleeping bag from getting wet at night. If it is a big tarp, position it so that a few of your group members can share. Then I would suggest putting a tarp over your sleeping bag when you go to sleep to prevent the dew from making your bag wet. Again, if your tarp is large, it could go over a few people's bags. I have seen some groups bring tents. They can be heavy and bulky to carry, but they do work just as well.

Once you have set up your area, take a look around. Where are the bathrooms? Where is the nearest exit? Where is the nearest medical tent? Where is the food? Before you go exploring, make sure you take a friend with you and tell your youth minister.

While in Sydney, I set up my things and went for a walk with other members of my group. When I came back, some things had been put right in front of my sleeping bag. I thought someone in my group was playing a joke. When I questioned this, someone from my group said it was Tonga. I said, "Who?" The members of my group had given each other nicknames during the week, and I was not sure who Tonga was. OK, again I asked who Tonga was. The teen said that a group from the country of Tonga had placed their things there. I said I had never heard of Tonga. I got out my map just as the people were coming back. We asked them to show us where their country was. For the next twenty-four hours, we had some new friends to sing with, dance with, eat with, and pray with. We learned about their culture and how they practice their Catholic faith in Tonga. Since World Youth Day, I have heard the country mentioned on TV shows and in the news.

In the last paragraph I mentioned a may. I had brought a map of the world to World Youth Day 2008 in Sydney. At previous World Youth Days, when I would meet people from other countries, sometimes I was not sure where they were located. Also, some people did not know where Connecticut was in the United States. So ast each World Youth Day when we met pilgrims, we would ask them where they were from and have them sign our map. We also took a picture of them. When we returned home, we matched up their pictures with their signatures and placed them on the map. We have a great keepsake that shows whom we met. We used one map for our group, and they copied it once we returned home. It was fun as we looked at the pictures and shared memories of our experiences with that person or group.

## Overnight

The weather for the overnight can be unpredictable. When we were in Cherry Creek Park in Denver, the temperature was over ninety degrees during the day, but dropped down to fifty degrees at night. After the pilgrimage, many were hot and sweaty. They were glad to sit and rest. But their clothes were damp, so as the temperature dropped, they began to get chilled. I would recommend changing into warm, dry clothes to sleep in if your clothes are sweaty.

In Toronto, the temperature was also hot. We were lucky to be near a fence, which we used to create a makeshift tent with a tarp to keep ourselves cool during the day. At night the temperature dropped, but we were prepared. What we were not prepared for was the sky opening up at five o'clock that morning and raining as hard as it could. The teens who did not want to get under the makeshift tent to keep cool when it was sunny, all wanted under it when it was pouring. Ten of us sat very close, with the tarp about

us. We had to create a system to drain the water off without getting our things wet. Luckily, right before the Saint Pope John Paul II was to arrive, the sky closed up and the sun came out. The temperatures then shot right up. That was great, because we were able to dry off our things before we had to leave.

In Sydney, since it was winter there, it was cool to begin with. We planned before we left and brought hats, gloves, scarves, hand warmers, and thermal blankets. We put tarps on the bottom of our sleeping bags and the tops to keep us warm. We also used hand warmers in our sleeping bags. OK, you want to know how we changed your clothes? Although each site has bathrooms, it may be a long wait. I would suggest just changing in your sleeping bag. It is part of the adventure.

In Madrid, the temperatures were also very, very warm. But God had a plan to cool us off. During the vigil he opened up the skies and brought rain down on all the pilgrims. Are you starting to see a pattern at the vigils? The big blue tarp came out once again and the pilgrims that were with us and all their things huddled under the tarp till the rain finished. One it was done pilgrims all came out from under their rain. I had worn jean shorts and they were drenched. I though oh no they are not going to ever dry and remembered I had brought a change of clothes. Well once the rain stopped we all had gotten up and were dancing, singing and worshiping. I forgot about my shorts being wet. When it came time hours later for me to get a bit of sleep in my sleeping bag I figured I would change the shorts. I touched the shorts and what do you know they were completely dry. God working this magic again.

One of the things on my bucket list was to one day sleep on a beach. In Rio that came true. Due to rain and flooding where we were to have the vigil it was not possible for the pilgrims to go there so they changed the site to Copacabana Beach. How cool to not only be able to sleep out on a beach but a real famous one. There were about 3 million others who shared in this awesome experience. In my book coming soon the Experiences from the Ultimate Pilgrimage for Catholic Youth I will share about the faces of Christ that I experienced on that beach.

## Meals

For the vigil, they usually give you a box with food for lunch, dinner, and breakfast. Sometimes they have stations for you to get your food at the site. In Germany, they had the best chicken and rice dinner. Make sure you keep yourself hydrated and well nourished.

✛ Journal: Once settled in your space at the pilgrimage site, take time to write about your experience so far in chapter 9 of your journal.

☼ *Tip: Today you need to have a lot of patience. Remember to drink water and pace yourself during the walk.*

✞ "Your word is a lamp for my feet, a light for my path." (Psalm 119:105)

# Chapter 10: Vigil

The overnight vigil will be an overwhelming experience. Once the Pope arrives, everyone will participate in a prayer service. In Denver, Toronto, Cologne and Krakow. The Pope lit a candle on the altar, and the flame was spread by youth who lit their candles from his and brought it to others in the crowd to pass along. The candle lighting service was awesome to see and experience, as the darkness slowly begins to light up for miles. Adoration will occur during the vigil and is a moving experience. Prayers will be said, and songs will be sung In Rio, the vigil was held on Copacabana beach. During adoration Matt Maher, a Contemporary Christian singer from Canada, sang the song " Lord I need you". It was very powerful to hear three million youth all singing and praising God on their knees together. There was also a time of silence and it was amazing with all those people it was quiet and the only sound you heard was the waves from the ocean. It was beautiful.

 Once the evening service is over, the Pope will leave, and the music and singing will continue through the night. You may not get much sleep, but this is a once-in-a-lifetime event. You can say a rosary with neighbors from another country and talk to other young people on how they practice their faith in their country.

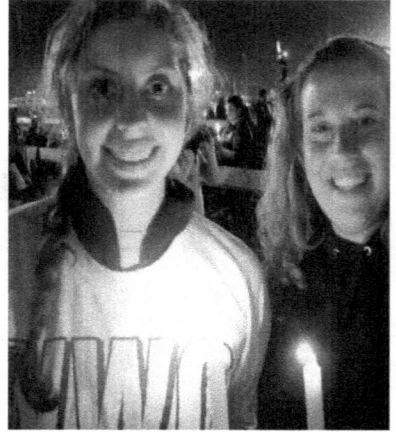

✦ Journal: Before you go to sleep, take out your flashlight and reflect on the vigil in the chapter 10 section of your journal.
☼ *Tip: As the vigil progresses, take each moment in. This is an awesome powerful experience.*

╬ "This is my commandment; love one another as I love you." (John 15:12)

# Chapter 11: Closing Mass

As the sun begins to rise, so will thousands of pilgrims. Members of the public will also be allowed to attend the closing Mass with the Pope.

I want to share with you one of my favorite parts of the closing Mass. It is when we say the "Our Father." It is the coolest sound to hear people from many different languages saying the same prayer in their native language. We speak many languages, but all share in the same belief of our God. You can go to www.sunshinelife.net to hear it during the closing Mass in Sydney.

Since thousands of people will be attending the closing Mass, Communion can take a while, but the organizers of WYD have hundreds of priests spread all around the site to give Communion.

At this Mass the Pope will also bless items that you have brought or bought. Three American flags from our parish have been blessed. One was blessed by Saint Pope John Paul II, the second by Pope Benedict and the third by Pope Francis. At the end of closing

Mass, the Pope will announce the location for the next World Youth Day.

## Leaving the Vigil Site

As you pack your things to leave the pilgrim site, take all the garbage and things that you brought in. Since thousands of people will all be trying to leave at the same time, your youth minister may have you hang back for awhile. You can read, catch up on some sleep, or meet other pilgrims that you have not met yet. Once you do start going, the roads, buses, and trains are going to be full with people. Have patience. Sing some songs. As we left from Ranwick Racecourse in Sydney, we met up with a young woman who had just received her confirmation from Pope Benedict. We were able to hear the story about her life and how she was a lucky person to be selected to have the Holy Father bestow her confirmation on her.

When we left the vigil in Germany, we had to walk a distance to get to a bus that would take us to our hotel. We were sharing this bus with a group from Michigan, so we had to wait until they got there. The driver had opened the lower compartments so we could sit in them and wait, since it was hot in the bus. We had waited for about an hour when one of the youths I was with poked me and said, "Look." It was the baby carriage with the lady it in, being pushed by a gentleman. The rest of the group I was with was able to see her. Things happen in threes, and this was the third time I saw this lady. I wondered why God had put in her my presence three times. I have reflected on this many times, and many things come to mind. One thing especially is that no matter how bad things are, have faith in God, and he will guide you through it; and be thankful for what you have. I often think of that woman and wish that I had spoken to her. I hope one day our paths cross again at a World Youth Day and I get to talk with her.

+ Journal: Before you go to sleep, reflect in the chapter 11 section of your journal about your experiences at the closing Mass.

☼ *Tip: Everyone will be tired and anxious to leave. Have patience and go with the flow.*

☩ "Sing to the LORD, bless his name; announce his salvation day after day." (Psalm 96:2)

# Chapter 12: Pre/Post World Youth Day Extensions

Either before or after World Youth Day, you may have opportunities to experience some of the culture and sites of the host country. When we went to World Youth Day in Cologne, Germany, we stayed an extra day and were able to take a cruise down the Rhine River and visit a castle. For World Youth Day in Australia, we went a few days earlier and were able to visit the Great Barrier Reef and take in all the beauty and splendor that it offers. We also were able to spend time with some native aboriginal people to learn about their culture and traditions. They welcomed us in and painted our faces in tribal designs and patterns. They even showed us how to throw a boomerang. I was not very good at it. It was to be thrown and come back to you. Mine just hit the ground. Oh, well. It was a lot of fun and a good laugh. They even taught us how to play some musical instruments and do a native dance.

When you think about Australia, you think about kangaroos, koalas, and the Sydney Opera House. We had the opportunity to go to the Taronga Zoo and see koalas and pet a kangaroo. We also were fortunate to go to a performance at the Sydney Opera House, where we saw a group of young musicians from Australia. What a fantastic group of young talent!

Before WYD in Madrid we landed in Portugal and visited St Anthony's Church and the location of his childhood home in Lisbon. St Anthony was my Grandma's and Mom's favorite saint. Growing up my grandparents had a huge St Anthony statue with white fence arch with flowers around in located in their backyard. When my grandparents passed my parents brought the statue to their house. It was quite special for me to visit this church and his home. We also were privileged to have mass there by the priests we were traveling with. The pilgrims I brought with me read and led the music at the mass.

After Lisbon we went to Fatima and were able to participate in the candlelight procession that they had. Then we proceed to Santiago de Compostela, Spain. The church I am from is called St James so it was exciting for us visit the Cathedral de Santiago de Compostela which is the burial site for St James. People from all over the world do Pilgrimages here. They know they arrived when they see the sea shell on the ground. Here are the feet of the members of the group I was with.

When we went to Rio for WYD we visited Corcovado Christ the Redeemer and Sugarloaf Mountain. Two very beautiful wonders of the world.

In Poland we visited Jasna Gora- The Shrine of Our Lady of Czestochowa- where we had the opportunity to celebrate mass in front of the Icon. ( to the left) We also went to Auschwitz-Birkenau which is the Former German Nazi Concentration and Extermination Camp. This was a very moving day to see all these youths from around the world respectfully and silently waling the grounds and reflecting on what happened there. I like to take pictures of me at different places I have been, but I struggled on how to take a picture of me there. When we take a picture you usually smile and that did not seem

appropriate to me. To the left is a picture of the train car that they used to transport the people. When we left there, we went to Wadowice which is the birthplace of Saint John Paul II. We visited the Minor Basilica of the Prestation of the Blessed Virgin Mary which is next door to John Paul II"s Family House Museum.

The final place we visited in Poland was Divine Mercy Sanctuary in Krakow which is the final resting place of Saint Faustina Kowalska. Jesus appeared to Saint Faustina as the painting is shown below and told her to paint a image like what she see with a the words "Jesus I trust in you"

We have some great memories and lessons to take back to families from each of our Pre and Post World Youth Day experiences.

+ Journal: Before you head to bed, go to chapter 12 of your journal and write about your excursions, as well as the places you went and the people you met.

☼ *Tip: Make sure you have the agenda for today and know where you are going. Also ask your youth minister where you will be meeting if someone gets lost. Always go with a buddy.*

"Stand and consider the wondrous works of God."    ( Job 37:14)

# Chapter 13: Going Home

Now it is time to pack everything up to go home. That extra bag I mentioned in the things to bring along can come in handy. Many airlines are now charging for extra bags. So, if you and a few group members put your extras into one or two bags, you can share the cost of the bag. Clean up your hotel room and leave a tip for the housekeeping staff.

You are right now on a spiritual high. You are pumped about your faith and eager to share it with others. Be prepared that folks at home may not be as excited as you are. They did not have the awesome experience that you have had, and they do not know how to relate to it. It will be your challenge to share your experiences and blessings with your family and friends. Don't give up. God does not give up on us.

✢ Journal: When you get home, go to chapter 13 of your journal to reflect on your day.

☼ *Tip: Thank God for the great experience that you had and all the blessings that he has given you.*

✠ "But as for you, be strong, and do not relax for your work shall be rewarded." (2 Chronicles 15:7)

# Chapter 14: A Month Later

Time has passed since you went on your World Youth Day pilgrimage. What did you learn that you are practicing now, and what are you sharing with others? Are there things you need help with concerning your faith? At your next youth group meeting, talk with others to see how they are taking what they learned and sharing it with others. Get together to share pictures and videos that you have taken.

+ Journal: Go to chapter 14 in your journal to reflect on how you have shared your World Youth Day experience with others.

☼ *Tip: Share your pictures and experiences with younger teens to get them excited about going to the next World Youth Day.*

✠ "God is with you in everything you do." (Genesis 21:22)

# Journal Questions

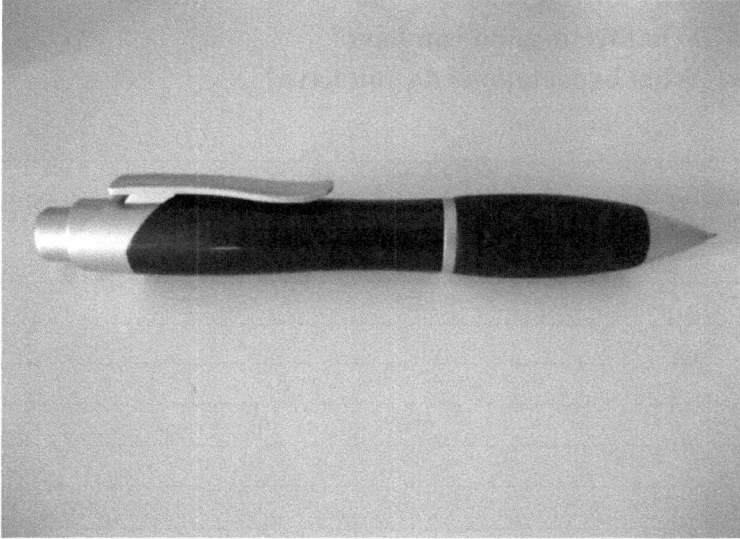

Welcome to your journal section. This section will become a valuable tool for you as you prepare for your pilgrimage and while you are on your pilgrimage. It will also help you to reflect after your pilgrimage.

Let's begin.

# Chapter 1: Preparing

**Date:** _____

- Why do you want to go to World Youth Day?
- What feelings do you have?
- What expectations do you have?

_____
_____
_____
_____
_____
_____
_____
_____
_____
_____
_____
_____
_____
_____
_____
_____
_____
_____
_____
_____
_____
_____
_____
_____

# Chapter 2: Fund-raising

**Date:** _____

- How much do you need to raise?
- What fund-raisers are you doing? (dates and times)
- Are you doing your part?

_____

_____

_____

_____

_____

_____

_____

_____

_____

_____

_____

_____

_____

_____

_____

_____

_____

_____

_____

_____

_____

_____

_____

_____

_____

# Chapter 3: Packing for My Trip

**Date:** _____

- ⁑ **What emotions am I feeling?**
- ⁑ **What is going through my head?**
- ⁑ **Do I have everything that I am going to need?**

_____

_____

_____

_____

_____

_____

_____

_____

_____

_____

_____

_____

_____

_____

_____

_____

_____

_____

_____

_____

_____

_____

_____

_____

_____

# Chapter 4: Ready to Go

**Date:** _____

- As we get ready to go, I feel...
- I am excited about...
- I am looking forward to...

_____
_____
_____
_____
_____
_____
_____
_____
_____
_____
_____
_____
_____
_____
_____
_____
_____
_____
_____
_____
_____
_____

# Chapter 5: Opening Ceremonies

**Date:** _____

**Before leaving for today, do I have:**

___ Water  ___ Credentials  ___ Meal tickets  ___ Ponchos

___ Medicine  ___ Backpack  ___ Sweatshirt

___ Items to trade  ___ Snacks  ___ Pens  ___ Money

✝ I felt _____ at opening ceremonies.

✝ My favorite thing today was…

✝ I saw Jesus today…

_____

_____

_____

_____

_____

_____

_____

_____

_____

_____

_____

_____

_____

_____

_____

_____

_____

# Chapter 6: Catechesis Day 1

**Date:** _____

**Before leaving for today, do I have:**

___ Water   ___ Credentials   ___ Meal tickets   ___ Ponchos

___ Medicine   ___ Backpack   ___ Sweatshirt

___ Items to trade   ___ Snacks   ___ Pens   ___ Money

+ **The message I took from the bishop's talk today was…**
+ **My favorite thing today was…**
+ **I saw Jesus today…**

_____

_____

_____

_____

_____

_____

_____

_____

_____

_____

_____

_____

_____

_____

_____

_____

# Chapter 6: Catechesis Day 2

**Date:** _____

**Before leaving for today, do I have:**

___ Water    ___ Credentials    ___ Meal tickets    ___ Ponchos

___ Medicine    ___ Backpack    ___ Sweatshirt

___ Items to trade    ___ Snacks    ___ Pens    ___ Money

✦ The message I took from the bishop's talk today was...
✦ My favorite thing today was...
✦ I saw Jesus today...

_____

_____

_____

_____

_____

_____

_____

_____

_____

_____

_____

_____

_____

_____

_____

_____

_____

_____

# Chapter 6: Catechesis Day 3

**Date:** _____

**Before leaving for today, do I have:**

___ Water ___ Credentials ___ Meal tickets ___ Ponchos

___ Medicine ___ Backpack ___ Sweatshirt

___ Items to trade ___ Snacks ___ Pens ___ Money

+ **The message I took from the bishop's talk today was...**
+ **My favorite thing today was...**
+ **I saw Jesus today...**

_____

_____

_____

_____

_____

_____

_____

_____

_____

_____

_____

_____

_____

_____

_____

_____

# Chapter 7: Pope's Arrival

**Date:** _____

**Before leaving for today do I have:**

___ Water   ___ Credentials   ___ Meal tickets   ___ Ponchos

___ Medicine   ___ Backpack   ___ Sweatshirt

___ Items to trade   ___ Snacks   ___ Pens   ___ Money

- The Pope's arrival today was....
- Today I met other pilgrims from...
- I saw Jesus today...

_____
_____
_____
_____
_____
_____
_____
_____
_____
_____
_____
_____
_____
_____
_____
_____
_____
_____

# Chapter 8: Stations of the Cross

**Date:** _____

**Before leaving for today, do I have:**

___ Water   ___ Credentials   ___ Meal tickets   ___ Ponchos

___ Medicine   ___ Backpack   ___ Sweatshirt

___ Items to trade   ___ Snacks   ___ Pens   ___ Money

✢ **When I saw the Stations of the Cross, I…**
✢ **I saw Jesus today…**

_____

_____

_____

_____

_____

_____

_____

_____

_____

_____

_____

_____

_____

_____

_____

_____

# Chapter 9: Pilgrimage

**Date:** _____

**Before leaving for today, do I have:**

___ Water   ___ Credentials   ___ Meal tickets   ___ Ponchos

___ Backpack   ___ Sweatshirt   ___ Items to trade   ___ Pens

___ Sleeping Bag   ___ Tarp   ___ Toothbrush/Paste

___Flashlight   ___ Change of clothes   ___ Medicine

___ Snacks   ___ Money   ___ Hats/Gloves

+ On today's pilgrimage…
+ I feel…
+ I saw Jesus today…

_____

_____

_____

_____

_____

_____

_____

_____

_____

_____

_____

_____

_____

_____

# Chapter 10: Vigil

**Date:** _____

- ✢ As I lie in my sleeping bag...
- ✢ As I reflect on today, I...
- ✢ I saw Jesus today...

_____

_____

_____

_____

_____

_____

_____

_____

_____

_____

_____

_____

_____

_____

_____

_____

_____

_____

_____

_____

_____

_____

_____

_____

_____

_____

_____

# Chapter 11: Closing Mass

**Date:** _____

**Before leaving for today, do I have:**

___ Water  ___ Credentials  ___ Meal tickets  ___ Ponchos

___ Backpack  ___ Sweatshirt  ___ Medicine

___ Items to trade  ___ Pens  ___ Money

___ All items I brought to the vigil  ___ Garbage to get rid of

- The message I took from the closing mass…
- As I reflect on today, I…
- I saw Jesus today…
- When I get home, I…

_____

_____

_____

_____

_____

_____

_____

_____

_____

_____

_____

_____

_____

_____

_____

# Chapter 12: Pre/Post WYD

## Day 1

**Date:** _____

**Before leaving for today, do I have:**

___ Water ___ Credentials ___ Ponchos ___ Medicine

___ Backpack ___ Sweatshirt ___ Items to trade ___ Pens

___ Money

- On today's excursion, I...
- As I reflect on today, I...
- I saw Jesus today...

_____

_____

_____

_____

_____

_____

_____

_____

_____

_____

_____

_____

_____

_____

_____

# Chapter 12: Pre/Post WYD

## Day 2

**Date:** _____

**Before leaving for today, do I have:**

___ Water    ___ Credentials    ___ Ponchos    ___ Medicine

___ Backpack    ___ Sweatshirt    ___ Items to trade

___ Pens    ___ Money

- On today's excursion, I…
- As I reflect on today, I…
- I saw Jesus today…

_____

_____

_____

_____

_____

_____

_____

_____

_____

_____

_____

_____

_____

_____

# Chapter 12: Pre/Post WYD

## Day 3

**Date:** _____

**Before leaving for today, do I have:**

___ Water ___ Credentials ___ Ponchos ___ Medicine

___ Backpack ___ Sweatshirt ___ Items to trade

___ Pens ___ Money

- On today's excursion, I...
- As I reflect on today, I...
- I saw Jesus today...

_____

_____

_____

_____

_____

_____

_____

_____

_____

_____

_____

_____

_____

_____

# Chapter 12: Pre/Post WYD

## Day 4

**Date:** _____

**Before leaving for today, do I have:**

___ Water ___ Credentials ____ Ponchos ___ Medicine

___ Backpack ___ Sweatshirt ___ Items to trade

___ Pens ___ Money

- On today's excursion, I…
- As I reflect on today, I…
- I saw Jesus today…

_____
_____
_____
_____
_____
_____
_____
_____
_____
_____
_____
_____
_____
_____
_____

# Chapter 12: Pre/Post WYD

## Day 5

**Date:** _____

**Before leaving for today, do I have:**

___ Water ___ Credentials ___ Ponchos ___ Medicine

___ Backpack ___ Sweatshirt ___ Items to trade

___ Pens ___ Money

- On today's excursion, I...
- As I reflect on today, I...
- I saw Jesus today...

_____

_____

_____

_____

_____

_____

_____

_____

_____

_____

_____

_____

_____

_____

# Chapter 13: Going Home

**Date:** _____

- ✦ Today I enjoyed…
- ✦ Some of my favorite memories we shared today…
- ✦ I saw Jesus today…

_____

_____

_____

_____

_____

_____

_____

_____

_____

_____

_____

_____

_____

_____

_____

_____

_____

_____

_____

_____

_____

_____

_____

_____

_____

# Chapter 14: A Month Later

**Date:** _____

- ✠ Today as I look back...
- ✠ I have shared my experiences from World Youth Day by...
- ✠ I saw Jesus today...

_____

_____

_____

_____

_____

_____

_____

_____

_____

_____

_____

_____

_____

_____

_____

_____

_____

_____

_____

_____

_____

_____

_____

_____

# Part 3: Youth Minister Guide to World Youth Day

©2011 Sharon M Gagne

# Introduction

As a fellow youth minister, I would like to thank you for being willing to take young people on a great spiritual journey which is World Youth Day. I know you are probably thinking that you are crazy, and the answer is, "*Yes*, you are!" You are crazy about Jesus and your Catholic faith, and you have the gift of helping young people learn and come closer to God. Throughout this section, I will give you tips on things that I have found helpful and things you should avoid when going to World Youth Day. One thing to remember when working with teens is that you have to have a sense of humor. For this, I thank you, on behalf of all the teens who have been blessed to have you as their youth minister.

As a youth minister, I have taken teens on several retreats and pilgrimages; and with each retreat and pilgrimage, you learn something new and something different.

I have written different parts and chapters of this book in different locations. I wrote while waiting for a plane with a three-hour delay, flying on several planes, and while dealing with a cold. I wrote on a snowed-in day and on a sunny beach in Florida.

At the beach one day, I watched a lady struggle to bring all her beach things down to the beach. She had chairs, towels, sand toys, and a cooler. Then out of the blue, someone came to help her carry what she needed and made her load light. There will be times on your World Youth Day pilgrimage that God will send extra hands to help you also.

## See you at the next World Youth Day!

### Sharon☺

# Chapter 15: Preparing

Where to start? Making arrangements for a World Youth Day pilgrimage can be an overwhelming experience. As you make plans for World Youth Day (WYD), make sure you find out all the details of the trip. Some of you will be making plans on your own, and some of you will be using a tour company. There are many tour companies out there. Ask other parishes which ones they used and which ones they would recommend. Then call and speak to the youth minister about the experience.

When working with a tour company, check for things that might not be included:

- Cost. Find out what is included in the cost: housing (hotel, house, hostel), WYD registration, airline tickets, airport fees, food. Also if you are doing a Pre/ Post WYD Excursion or participating in Days of the Diocese.
- Deposits & Payment. When is the deposit due? Is it refundable? Is it transferrable? When will the payments be due?
- Tips & Fees. Find out what is included and what is not.
- Food & Beverages. Some places meals are included, but the beverages are not. A pitcher of water is usually available, if there is no problem with the local drinking

water. If you have any doubts about the safety of the drinking water, have your teens bring their water bottles to their meals with them to save money. If not, you may have to have them buy bottled water.

- Travel Insurance. The cost is not usually that much, and it will be well worth it if something happens and someone needs to cancel at the last minute. We had a young man break his arm the week before we were going to Poland.

- Local Cell Phone. Make sure your tour company gives you a cell phone to use in the country that you are in. Your own cell phone may work there, but the charges will be expensive. You may need to call the tour company to make sure your bus is coming or to get in touch with your tour company.

**Things also to do:**

- Passport & Visa. If World Youth Day is out of the country, you will need to obtain a passport. It can take several weeks or months to get one. Once your pilgrims have committed to go, I would encourage them to get a passport. It is important to make sure they are valid for six months from your return date, in case you need to extend your stay due to an emergency. Some countries require you to get a visa also. Check with the country you are traveling to.

- Registering for World Youth Day. Once you know who is going, get their information right away. You will need the following: name, address, phone number, birthday, &

e-mail information. You will also need a copy of their passport information.

- Support Systems. Find out from your tour company what supports systems you will have along the way and once you get to World Youth Day.

  ✓ Will they pick up your registration packets at World Youth Day, or do you need to do that?
  ✓ Will the tour company have a representative on site at World Youth Day?
  ✓ Will they be meeting you at the airport?
  ✓ Will they be providing you with transportation, or are you using public transportation?
  ✓ Will they provide a translator?

✠ Journal: As you prepare for World Youth Day, go to chapter 1 in the journal and reflect on your preparations.

☼ *Tip: Have the contact name and number of your tour company with you at all times while at World Youth Day. You never know when you might need them.*

✠ "Trust in the LORD with all your heart on your own intelligence rely not; In all your ways be mindful of him and he will make straight your paths." (Proverbs 3:5-6)

Tour Company Question Checklist

| | |
|---|---|
| *Tour company* | |
| *Cost* | |
| *Payments & Dates* | |
| *Housing* | |
| *WYD registration* | |
| *Transportation* | |
| *Tips & Fees* | |
| *Food* | |
| *Travel Insurance* | |

*© 2011,2016,2018 Sharon M. Gagne*

# Chapter 16: Fund-raising

As a youth minister, it seems like I am always doing fund-raising. We have tried several different types of fund-raisers in my parish. Some work, while others do not. We have sold sweatshirts and T-shirts with our church's name on the front and a Bible quote on the back. They were very successful. People are proud of their church and like to share that. I then asked parishioners if there were other things they would like with the church name on it. Many said travel coffee mugs. We placed an order for those, but that did not go as well. I still have several cases of the mugs. We have sold them at every event we have had for the past few years. The cases seem to grow every time I go to the closet where they're kept.

Another item that we found difficult to sell was candy. The youth are all involved in many other things, such as sports teams, dance groups, and Boy and Girl scouts. Most of them sell candy as a major fund-raiser, so you don't want to compete.

One thing to remember is to involve the parents or guardians of the youths who are going. As the person coordinating this pilgrimage, you have lot of things that need to be done behind the scenes; running all the fund-raisers on top of that can be overwhelming. Ask for help.

+ Journal: As you are fund-raising, write about what you are doing and how it is going in chapter 2 of the journal.

☼ *Tip: Keep a chart showing which teens help and when, so that everyone does an equal amount.*

✠ "Seek first the Kingdom of God and his righteousness, and all these things added on to you." (Matthew 6:33)

**Fund-raiser checklist**

| Fundraiser:_____ | | |
|---|---|---|
| **Pilgrims' names** | **Helped** | **Did not help** |
| | | |
| | | |
| | | |
| | | |
| | | |
| | | |
| | | |
| | | |
| | | |
| | | |

*©2011 ,2016,2018 Sharon M. Gagne*

# Chapter 17: What to Pack

Packing for World Youth Day can be a lot of fun, but it can also be frustrating. In chapter 3 of the youth section, I have a list of items they should bring. Here I have listed some additional items that the youth minister should do and bring. You may be laughing at some of the items, but when they come in handy, you will be thanking me.

Once it is packed, put a check in the Sun ☼

- ☼ **First Aid Kit.** Carry with you each day. Pack scissors and nail clippers in your luggage, not in your carry-on.
- ☼ **Feminine Hygiene Products**. Put a few in the first aid kit.
- ☼ **Instant Ice Packs.** Pack a few of them.
- ☼ **Duct Tape.** I used it many times, for taping up bags, shoes, boxes, and for making a bra strap in a pinch.
- ☼ **Glow Bracelets**. They are great for keeping track of your group at night.
- ☼ **T-shirts.** I would recommend having T-shirts with your church name on them and in colors that stand out. This way you can spot one another in a crowd. I had a participant on one of my pilgrimages who was colorblind, and we chose colors that he could see.
- ☼ **Copies of All Passports, Medical Forms, & Visas**. Keep these in a binder. Make a note of all allergies and medical conditions. Check with participants to see if you can share their medical info with others in your group. You may not be with your youths at every moment. If you have someone who is diabetic and may have a reaction, it is better for the group to know in advance how to help him or her, in case

that person needs it. It is better to be prepared and not need it.

Food allergies are another thing. You are going to a foreign country and will be trying new things. Many people are allergic to seafood, dairy, and eggs. Many people also have celiac disease. Know what your youths can and cannot have and what to do if they encounter those items. Remind teens to advocate for themselves by asking what is in a food item before they eat it. Also find out who is vegetarian and vegan

**Leave a copy of all emergency forms, paperwork, passports, and visas at your church in case of emergency.**

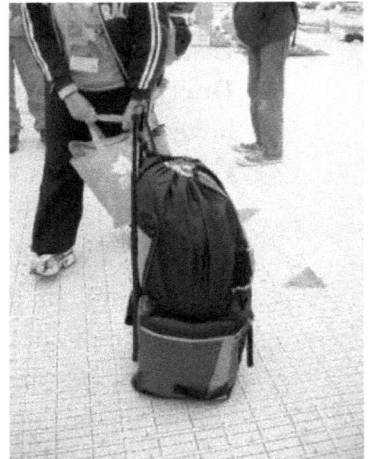

☼ **Foldable Rolling Cooler.** I have found this to be helpful in carrying things for the day, such as extra water, snacks, and so forth. When it is empty, it just folds up.

☼ **Flash Drive**. I also found that putting all the documents on a flash drive was easier to carry on a daily basis than the binder with all the forms in it. I left the binder in a safe at the hotel so I could easily get it in an emergency. I carried the flash drive with me each day. I also got a waterproof pouch to put it in, because you are never sure of the weather conditions. Purchase one at a local outdoors store.

- ☼ **Flag from Your Country.** Display this on a pole for all to see
- ☼ **Business Cards with Important Info.** Create business-size cards for the kids to carry on them with their flight info, hotel info, and contact info. These can easily be put in a wallet.
- ☼ **Itinerary for Family.** Make sure parents have a copy of the info and the itinerary.
- ☼ **Paper & Envelopes.** Bring paper and an envelope for each pilgrim to write a letter to themselves at the vigil. You will collect them and send the letter back to them a month later.
- ☼ **Notarized Forms.** To travel out of the country with teens, you will need notarized permission from their parents. Your diocese will have a form for you. Do this a few months before you go. You will need permission from both parents. If you have pilgrims whose parents are divorced you will need to find out if they have joint custody and have both parents sign the form. We had one parent who was a truck driver and was on the road traveling a lot. Therefore, special plans had to be made.
- ☼ **Send-off Mass.** Get your pilgrims, families, and parishioners together for a send-off mass. Have your priest give your pilgrims a special blessing.

✦ Journal: As you pack, go to the chapter 3 section of your journal and reflect on the experience.

☼ *Tip: If other chaperones are going with you, share carrying the first aid kit with them, or put it in the rolling cooler. Have each member of your group take turns pulling the cooler.*

☩ "I can do all things through Him who strengthens me." (Philippians 4:13)

# Chapter 18: Getting Ready to Depart

A few months before you go, contact your local paper, Catholic newspaper, or television station about the pilgrimage that your teens are about to go on. Have them interview the students before they go and when they return. This is a nice way for the community to see what the teens in the area are doing, and it gives the teens a way to share their faith with the community.

## Communication Home

❖ Before you leave, I recommend setting up a phone chain. When you arrive at your destination, call the first person on the list and let him or her know you have arrived. Have that person begin the phone tree. Have the last person call the first person to make sure everyone got the message. Make sure each contact person knows that depending on where you are traveling to, the arrival time may be earlyin the morning or late at night. So, the first person should expect a call at any time, and should call the next person on the phone chain right away. If no one answers, that person should go to the next name on the list but continue to call the person till he or she gets the message.

❖ Another option is to send a mass e-mail. Remember that you will be busy each day and will not have much time to use a computer; and computer time can be expensive. A week before you leave, run a test to make sure all numbers and e-mails work.

❖ Remind parents that they should only call or contact you in an emergency. Tell parents to be aware of the time change from country to country. I was woken up at three o'clock in the morning by a hotel staff with the message that one of my teens needed to call home. I woke her up, and we went to find a phone to make out-of-country calls. When we got in touch with the parents to see what the emergency was, was no emergency. It was just to say hi. *Aaahhh*!

## On the Day You Leave:

Before you leave your church, check with your teens to make sure they all have the necessary things they need. Ask to personally see each person's passport and visa. When I was going to Toronto,

we were on the bus getting ready to go when one teen remembered she changed her pants right before she left and left her passport at home. Luckily, her home was not that far away, and her parents were able to run to get it. Also make sure they have some money with them. At our first rest stop, that same teen realized that all her money was in those pants that she had changed. Fortunately, I had brought along a credit card, so I was able to charge her expenses while we were at World Youth Day, and her parents were able to reimburse me on our return.

## Traveling With Youth

So, you may ask, what is the best way to get your pilgrims on a bus or train and make sure they are all there? Here is what I did. It has seemed to work at the last seven World Youth Days and several regional conferences. Before we arrive at WYD I give each of my pilgrims a number. I start with me and gave myself number one and then continued through all pilgrims and chaperones. I made sure the last person was a chaperone. Then I had each person line up in order and take a look at who was on each side of them. I asked each of them to count off in order. I expressed the importance of paying attention to the voice of the person before them and after them. I told them this was important because when we are on a train or a bus, I will call out the name of our church and ask them to count off. Sometimes you might not be able to see that person, but you will be able to hear his voice. It would go like this: I would say "Saint James, count off, one." I would listen for each number to be called, then listen for my last chaperone's voice. The teens may think this is silly at first, but you will find them asking you to count off to make sure that everyone is there. They take it seriously.

## Traveling on a Plane or Bus

Sometimes your journey can be long. If you travel by bus, I recommend bringing appropriate movies for your teens to watch. Encourage your teens to bring along books and travel games. At a youth group meeting, talk with your teens about what they think they might bring. If they bring a variety of books and games, everyone can share.

If your group travels by plane, they can still bring books and games, but they need to be aware of the weight of the items. Luggage has weight restrictions, so check with your airline. While flying, if it is a long distance, encourage your pilgrims to get up and walk around so that their blood circulates. Make sure they drink water to keep themselves hydrated.

## Customs

Before you land, you will be given customs paperwork. Be sure your pilgrims complete the paperwork before leaving the plane. It will make going through customs easier. Remind teens it can take awhile and to be patient.

## Locating Bags & Suitcases

I went to a local travel store and bought big, bright, smiley-face name tags. I had all the travelers in our group put one on their bags. When we are in baggage claim, our group would position ourselves around the luggage belt and pull off the bags that had the orange tags on them. This made the process go smoothly. Make sure each pilgrim's bags are claimed before you leave. If a bag is lost, take that pilgrim to the nearest airline representative.

When we arrived in Brisbane, Australia, one of the pilgrim's bags were missing. Since we were connecting to a domestic flight in Australia, I sent the rest of the group ahead with a chaperone. They could tell the gate agent what happened and to hold the flight for us. The airline was helpful and issued a money voucher for the pilgrim to buy some clothes for the next day. The luggage had been left in Los Angeles and would take another day to get there.

## **Upon Arrival at the Hotel**

Once you arrive at your hotel, go in first to check in your group. Get keys and room assignments. Make sure you have a list of your teens and where their rooms are located. Make sure your youths know which room yours is. Check out their rooms to make sure they are OK, and nothing is damaged in the room. If something is damaged or missing, let hotel staff know before the teens go to their rooms.

When we were in Canada, they put some of my youths on a smoking floor. One student had severe asthma and could not be there. It took some negotiating with the front desk, but I was able to move all my teens to non-smoking floors. Many hotels are non-smoking now, which may help.

## World Youth Day Packets

You will receive your World Youth Day bags with your credentials, meal tickets, book and guide for the week, and lots of other goodies. Depending on your arrangements with your tour company, they may have them delivered right to your hotel for you. If not, you will have go to the World Youth Day headquarters to pick up your things. Stress with your youth the importance of the credentials. Make sure the teens do not lose them. They will also get their event tickets for the week and the tickets for food.

Before you leave your hotel each day, check your teens for their credentials, hotel information, and meal tickets. Ask to visually see them. I had a teen say yes when I asked if he had his meal tickets, but when it was time to eat, he did not have them. Fortunately, all the pilgrims had enough food that they could share. From that day on, I asked each pilgrim to show me the meal tickets and credentials.

✚ Journal: As your day winds down, journal in chapter 4 about the adventures you had today.

☼ *Tip: Sometimes travel plans do not go as smoothly as you would like. Remain calm and go with the flow.*

✝ "It is more blessed to give than to receive." (Acts 20:35)

# Chapter 19: Opening Ceremony

☼ Before you leave your hotel, check your journal to see what you need to bring with you today.

## Opening Ceremonies

As the youth minister, assign your group a common meeting spot in case someone gets lost. Make sure your teens always go with at least another person when they get something to eat, mingle with others, and go to the restrooms. As you are waiting for events to start, mingle with other youth ministers from other countries. Get to know them. See what they do with their youth groups.

## World Youth Day Meals

The food selections vary from World Youth Day to World Youth Day. Encourage your teens to try something new. Bring along snacks for those picky eaters so they can keep themselves fueled. Remind youth to continuously drink water all day.

## Reconciliation

At the opening ceremony venue, there usually is a place for Reconciliation for you and your youth, if you wish. You will have opportunities to go each day at the different venues. The lines may be long. Be encouraging to your teens and offer to go with them if they are nervous about it. If needed, remind them about the examination of conscious and how to go to confession. Have them look at the guide in Appendix E.

## Restrooms

If your youth need to use the restrooms, the lines are usually long, but I have found that waiting in line can be fun. Here is an opportunity to meet a lot of people from many different countries and strike up great conversations. Send them with that handy roll of toilet paper that you have been carrying in your backpack.

You will see and experience a lot of cool things. There will be a lot of miracles and works of Jesus around you.

✠ Journal: Before you turn in tonight, journal in chapter 5 about your experiences at the opening ceremonies and reflect on the ways you have seen Jesus today.

☼ *Tip: One way to keep your teens together when moving in a crowd is to form a line and hold onto the backpack in front of you. Have someone holding your flag or banner at the beginning of the line so you can all see it.*

✠ "I will instruct you and show you the way you should walk, give you counsel and watch over you." (Psalm 32:8)

# Chapter 20: Catechesis & Day 1, 2, & 3 & Youth Festivals

☼ Before you leave your hotel, check your journal to see what you need to bring.

When you get your World Youth Day packet, you will be assigned a catechesis site for three days. Each catechesis day will be different. They usually are from 9:00 a.m. to 1:00 p.m. You can expect music, speakers, skits, and readings. A bishop will talk about the theme of the day. Once he is done speaking, expect a question and answer session, followed by Mass. Sometimes there is adoration. You will have your lunch for this day at your site.

In Sydney, Madrid, Rio, and Krakow. I had the privilege of leading catechesis for three days. It was an awesome experience. Since Sydney was the first one I did, a great deal of work went into preparing for it. I am thankful for twenty-eight hours of plane rides to get there. We did a lot of planning on the planes. One thing we did is to prepare skits. We had skits planned for two of the three days of catechesis. On the night before the last catechesis, the youth who were with me asked if we could do another skit. We read and rehearsed it at midnight the night before. I read the skit, and the group that was with me acted it out. We were tired but did our best to rehearse. The next day, during the skit, the teens were quite funny with their acting, which made me start to laugh while I was reading. I even had to pause several times to laugh. We finally made it through it, and it turned out well.

When going to catechesis, remind your teens to go with an open mind and heart, and they will be amazed what God has in store for them.

**Youth Festivals**

In the afternoon you will be attending youth festivals. As the youth minister, ask your teens to look things over and get a consensus of what interests them. You know your group and the needs of your group. Many of the performances are at several times and places. If you cannot make a performance one day, try it another day.

Sometimes, as we were headed to an event, we would stumble on other things. In Germany we found a church having adoration in the lower catacombs. When we went down there, the monstrance was there, with a single rose placed near it. This church was an amazing church, and many people in our group had some kind of experience in it. If we didn't stop and pop in, we never would have had this awesome experience. Flexibility is very important.

## Evening Prayer

Each night try to get your group together for evening prayer. Set aside a time for them to process the day that they have had. I know many are tired; I had some teens fall asleep sitting up. But do try to pray and reflect on the day.

- Journal: As you wrap up each day of catechesis, reflect on the message from the bishops for that day. Write about the youth festivals you attended and how they made you feel. In conclusion write about how you saw Jesus today in chapter 6 of your journal.

☼ *Tip: You will meet people from different cultures who have different cultural expectations—personal space, for example. One of the volunteers would stand close to me when she would talk. I joked with her, "Oh, you are in my bubble." I then explained a bubble is the personal space around you. She said, "Oh, sorry, I sometimes get too close when I talk to someone."*

⳨ "Let us bow down in worship; let us kneel before the Lord who made us." (Psalm 95:6)

# Chapter 21: Arrival of the Pope

Today will be crowded. You will want to get to your site early to get a good spot. You may need to travel by bus, train, and on foot. In your World Youth Day registration packet, you will find a guidebook that tells you where the Pope's arrival will be. Have a plan with your teens in case you get separated from one another. Have your banner or flag on a high stick or pole for your teens to see.

Once you get to your spot, if outside, lay down a tarp and have your pilgrims put their things on it. Encourage your teens to mingle with youths from around the world. They can teach them a song from your country or even a game.

When the Pope is about to arrive, the crowd will begin to get loud and excited. When Saint Pope John Paul II was coming for WYD, the crowd was chanting, "JPII, we love you." Once the Pope reached a microphone, he said back to the crowd, "JPII, He... loves you." The youths went wild clapping and cheering. When Pope Benedict was arriving, the youth were chanting "Bennedicto" and clapping." In Rio when Pope Francis came the youth were chanting " Papa Francisco"

+ Journal: Reflect in chapter 7 of the journal on what it was like seeing the Pope for the first time.

☼ *Tip: Get a copy of the local paper. They will have great stories about WYD. Take only the articles about WYD so you don't have to carry the heavy paper home.*

       ✠ "Stand still and consider the wondrous works of God." (Job 37:14)

# Chapter 22: Stations of the Cross

Your World Youth Day Packet will tell you where the Stations of the Cross will be located. During some world youth days they had them spread throughout the city, and those involved move from one spot to another. Big screens are often set up around the city so that you can see the other stations from your spot.

✚ Journal: Reflect in chapter 8 about your feelings after viewing the Stations of the Cross.

☼ *Tip: Volunteers will help you find where you need to go.*

✚ "The LORD bless you and keep you." (Numbers 6:24)

# Chapter 23: Pilgrimage

As your group starts out on this pilgrimage walk, make sure everyone is walking with someone, and try to keep your group together. You will be given a map of the route you will need to walk. One suggestion is to have a person in front carry a pole with your church banner on it, or a flag from your country so that your group can see it.

The number of miles has differed from one World Youth Day to another. Remind your group to take breaks. Backpacks can get heavy, and your group has been walking all week. Fill your rolling cart with water bottles, fruit, and granola bars so that they have food to eat during the journey. Ask your group members to each take turns pulling the cooler.

Once you arrive at the vigil site, volunteers will direct you where to go. The vigil site is huge, and youth can easily get confused about where they are. Have each person in your group write down what section you are in. See if you can find a way to put the pole with your church banner or flag on it high so that your group can easily see it as they go where the food and restrooms are located. Another idea is to tie a battery light or a glow stick to the top of the pole so you can see it at night.

When you have found your spot, have each person set up his or her area with tarps and sleeping bags. Remind the teens that thousands of young people will be sleeping here, so things can get crowded if they don't have their things set out before the next group comes.

Get yourself and your youth orientated to where things are:
bathrooms, medical tents, food, and so forth. Make sure no one
leaves your area
alone.

(Right) Sharon
signing a cross
that was presented
to Pope Benedict.

+ Journal: Once you get to the site, reflect on your journey
here with your group in chapter 9 of the journal.

☼ *Tip: Talk with your group about the pace of your walk.
Your group should be as fast as your slowest walker.*

╫ "Ask and it will be given to you; seek
and you will find; knock and the door
will be opened to you." (Matthew 7:7)

# Chapter 24: Vigil

This evening will be a solemn moment. It is amazing to see how quiet and reverent a thousand youths are during this vigil.

After the Pope leaves for the night, more music and singing will take place. You may not get much sleep. Make sure your teens are dressed warm or cool enough for the evening's temperature.

At this point, give your teens the paper and envelopes you brought; encourage them to write themselves a letter about their experiences. Collect the letters and mail them to the teens a month after you return home.

⚜ Journal: Reflect on your evening in chapter 10.

☼ *Tip: If a youth needs to use the restroom during the night, make sure they wake up an adult to let them know, and have them take a friend with them.*

✠ "But if we walk in the light as he is in the light, then we have fellowship with one another, and the blood of his son Jesus cleanses us all from sin." (1 John 1:7)

# Chapter 25: Closing Mass

In the morning, the crowd will get bigger, since locals are invited to attend the Mass. In Sydney some nice folks sat near us. They had brought food with them, and they shared cookies with us. We tried to share some of our canned tuna with them, but they were not as excited about tuna as we were about their cookies.

This Mass will be the largest Mass that you will attend. I would encourage you to have your youth have their radios available. The mass will be broadcast on a channel in your language. That information is usually found in your World Youth Day book.

Once the Mass is over, you will begin to see a mass exodus. I would encourage you to have your group hang out at the pilgrimage site for a while, if you can. Thousands of pilgrims are getting on the buses, boats, and trains to go back to their hotels. Instead of standing for hours waiting in line for your transportation, wait at the site until some of the crowd has cleared out. It will make the journey back to your hotel easier. This can be a good time to process with your pilgrims about the last twenty-four hours and the experiences that they had with the pilgrimage, vigil, and the closing Mass.

✦ Journal: Once you get back to your sleeping accommodations, take time to reflect about today in chapter 11 of your journal.

☼ *Tip: Everyone will be tired and sore. When you reach your accommodations, encourage your pilgrims to go to bed early and get a good night's sleep. You will have fewer grumpies in the morning.*

✝ "Rejoicing in the LORD is your strength." (Nehemiah 8:10)

# Chapter 26: Going Home

As you are getting ready to leave your accommodations, check the following:

- ❖ As pilgrims pack to go home, have them share those extra duffle bags to take home any souvenirs that they have bought. Remember, some airlines charge for extra luggage.
- ❖ Check each pilgrim's room to be sure nothing has been left behind.
- ❖ Make sure your pilgrims have left a tip for the housekeeper at your hotel.
- ❖ Ask to see each pilgrim's passport before you leave your accommodations. You do not want to get to the airport to find out they cannot leave because they don't have their passport.

✠ Journal: Reflect on your travels back home in chapter 12 of the journal.

☼ *Tip: When you get home, contact a local newspaper and Catholic TV station to interview your teens about their experiences. They will be on a great high about their trip and will have a lot to share with others.*

> ✠ "To do your will is my delight; my God, your law is in my heart!" (Psalm 40:9)

# Chapter 27: Pre/Post World Youth Day Excursions

We have done both pre-World Youth Day and post-World Youth Day extensions. I prefer the pre-World Youth Day ones for several reasons. First, it gives the youth traveling together a time get to know one another before World Youth Day. Second, it gives them a chance to learn about and experience some of the country and the culture of the host country before WYD. Finally, World Youth Day is jam-packed with events all week, and you are on the go all the time. After the closing Mass, you will want your youths to rest and reflect on the week. We usually stay an extra day to do this.

In Sydney we did pre-World Youth Day excursions. We went to the Great Barrier Reef, met with aboriginal people, and took a walk in the rain forest. We did have some snags in our excursions, and I had to spend some time on the cell phone with our tour company. I was able to work some of it out, but not all. You live and learn, that's for sure. In Madrid, we went to Lisbon, Fatima, Santiago and Avila. In Rio we visited Corcovado and Sugar Loaf Mountain. In Krakow we went to Jansa Gora The Shrine of Our Lady of Czestochowa, Auschuwitz-Birkenau, Wadowice and Divine Mercy Shrine. Those were all awesome and powerful experiences.

+ Journal: Reflect on your pre/post World Youth Day excursion in chapter 13 of the journal.

☼ *Tip: Confirm each step of your excursions with the tour company before going.*

✠ "Cast all your worries upon him because he cares for you." (1 Peter 5:7)

# Chapter 28: A Month Later

At this time, send your pilgrims the letters they wrote at the vigil. Then schedule a youth group meeting for them a week after they receive the letters. Tell your pilgrims to bring their pictures and things to share.

✚ Journal: Reflect on getting together with your pilgrims a month after you have returned from your World Youth Day experience.

☼ *Tip: Invite parents and your priest to share in the pictures and experiences.*

╬ "Give thanks to God, bless his name, good indeed is the LORD, Whose love endures forever, whose faithfulness lasts through every age." (Psalm 100:4-5)

# Appendix A

## Previous International World Youth Days

### Locations, Themes, and Songs

### 1987 Buenos Aries, Argentina, April 11–12

"We ourselves have known and put our faith in God's love toward ourselves." (1 John 4:16)

Song: "Un Nuevo Sol"

### 1989 Santiago de Compostela, Spain, August 15–20

"I am the Way, the Truth and the Life." (John 14:6)

Song: "Somos Los Jóvenes"

### 1991 Czestochowa, Poland, August 10–15

"You have received a spirit of sonship." (Romans 8:15)

Song: "Abba Ojcze"

## 1993 Denver, USA, August 10–15

"I came that they might have life, and have it to the full." (John 10:10)

Song: "We Are One Body"


## 1995 Manila, Philippines, January 10–15

"As the Father sent me, so am I sending you," (John 20:21)

Song: "Tell the World of His Love"


## 1997 Paris, France, August 19–24

"Teacher, where are you staying? Come and see." (John 1:38-39)

Song: "Maître Et Seigneur"


## 2000 Rome, Italy, August 15–20

"The Word became flesh and dwelt among us." (John 1:14)

Song: "Emmanuel"

## 2002 Toronto, Canada, July 23–28

"You are the salt of the earth...You are the light of the world." (Matthew 5:13-14)

Song: "Lumière Du Monde/Light of the World"


## 2005 Cologne, Germany, August 16–21

"We have come to worship him." (Matthew 2:2)

Song: "Eum"


## 2008 Sydney, Australia, July 15–20

"You will receive power when the Holy Spirit comes upon you; and you will be my witnesses." (Acts 1:8)

Song: "Receive the Power"


## 2011 Madrid, Spain, August16- 21

"Rooted and Built Up in Jesus Christ, Firm in the Faith"

(Colossians 2:7)

Song: "Firmes en la Fe"

## 2013 Rio de Janerio, Brazil   July 23–28

"Go and make disciples of all nations "

(Matthew 28:19)

Song: "Hope of the Morning "

## 2016  Krakow, Poland, July 25- 31

"Blessed are the merciful, for they will receive mercy "

(Matthew 5:7)

Song: " Blessed Are The Merciful"

## 2019 Panama City, Panama  January 22-27

"I am the servant of the Lord. May It be done to me according to your word."

(Luke 1:38)

Song: "Behold the handmaid of the Lord, let it be done to me according to your word,"

# Appendix B

## Traded Items

| Item I Received | Country |
|---|---|
| | |
| | |
| | |
| | |
| | |
| | |
| | |
| | |
| | |
| | |
| | |
| | |
| | |
| | |
| | |
| | |
| | |
| | |
| | |
| | |
| | |
| | |
| | |
| | |
| | |

# Appendix C

# Pilgrims I Met

Pilgrim's Name                              Country

# Appendix D

# Prayers

## Our Father

Our Father, Who art in heaven
Hallowed be Thy Name;
Thy kingdom come,
Thy will be done,
on earth as it is in heaven.
Give us this day our daily bread,
and forgive us our trespasses,
as we forgive those who trespass against us;
and lead us not into temptation,
but deliver us from evil. Amen.

## Hail Mary

Hail Mary, full of grace.
Our Lord is with thee.
Blessed art thou among women,
and blessed is the fruit of thy womb,
Jesus.
Holy Mary, Mother of God,
pray for us sinners,
now and at the hour of our death.
Amen.

## Glory Be Prayer

Glory be to the Father and to
the Son and to the Holy Spirit,
as it was in the beginning, is now
and ever shall be, world without
end.

Amen.

# Resources

## Travel

American Automobile Association, www.aaa.com

Federal Aviation Administration, http://www.faa.gov/

The Weather Channel, http://www.weather.com/

United States Embassy, http://www.usembassy.gov/

## Fund-raising

Jewelry & Rosaries, www.totallycatholicfundraising.com

## Religious Resources

US Conference of Catholic Bishops, http://www.usccb.org/ wyd

The Vatican, www.vatican.va

# References

*Fireside Catholic Youth Bible* (2004). Wichita: Fireside Catholic Publishing.

Hunter, R. (2008). *World Youth Day Sydney 2008 Official Souvenir Guide.* Lane Cove: Event Merchandise Group.

Schmadebeck, R. (2003). Retrieved 2011, from World Youth Day: http://iml.jou.ufl.edu/projects/Spring03/Schmadebeck/logo.htm.

United States Conference of Catholic Bishops. Retrieved 2011, from http://www.usccb.org/wyd.

Webster (1989). *Webster's Ninth New Collegiate Dictionary.* Springfield: Merriam-Webster Inc.

# The Ultimate Pilgrimage for Catholic Youth

## *Order Form*

_____ Ultimate Pilgrimage for Catholic Youth

### Plus, cost of Shipping

Sunshine~Life—Sharon M. Gagne
P.O. Box 1084
Glastonbury, CT 06033

www.sunshinelife.net

**Please make checks payable to:**
Sunshine~Life—Sharon M. Gagne

Question: E-mail:

info@sunshinelife.net

# Watch for Sharon's next book:

## Experiences from the Ultimate Pilgrimage for Catholic Youth

## By: Sharon Gagne

Read more about Sharon's experiences from her World Youth Day pilgrimages. Also, inspirational stories and experiences from other pilgrims who she traveled with or met along the way.

Check out

www.sunslinelife.net for the release date.

---

# See you at
# World Youth Day!
# Sharon ☺